Langston Hughes was bor
1901. Often called 'The P
and edited over thirty works of poetry, novels, plays,
essays and children's books. He was a poetic innovator
and a central figure of the Harlem Renaissance, and
his writing promoted equality, condemned racism and
injustice and helped shape American literature and
politics. He died on May 22, 1967, in New York City.

Danez Smith is the author of four poetry collections
including *Bluff*, *Homie* and *Don't Call Us Dead*. Danez
has won the Forward Prize for Best Collection, the
Minnesota Book Award in Poetry, the Lambda
Literary Award for Gay Poetry and has been a finalist
for the NAACP Image Award in Poetry, the National
Book Critics Circle Award and the National Book
Award. Danez lives in Minneapolis with their people.

# BLUES IN STEREO

## The EARLY WORKS of
# LANGSTON
# HUGHES

## 1921–1927

Curated by Danez Smith

dialogue
books

DIALOGUE BOOKS

First published in the United States in 2024 by Legacy Lit,
an imprint of Grand Central Publishing
First published in Great Britain in 2024 by Dialogue Books

1 3 5 7 9 10 8 6 4 2

A CIP catalogue record for this book
is available from the British Library.

Paperback ISBN 978-1-408-77325-3

Typeset in Baskerville MT Std by Bart Dawson
Printed and bound in Great Britain by
Clays Ltd, Elcograf S.p.A

Papers used by Dialogue Books are from well-managed forests
and other responsible sources.

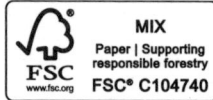

Dialogue Books
An imprint of Dialogue
Carmelite House
50 Victoria Embankment
London EC4Y 0DZ

www.dialoguebooks.co.uk

Dialogue, part of Little, Brown Book Group Limited,
an Hachette UK company.

So I am ashamed for the black poet who says, "I want to be a poet, not a Negro poet," as though his own racial world were not as interesting as any other world. I am ashamed, too, for the colored artist who runs from the painting of Negro faces to the painting of sunsets after the manner of the academicians because he fears the strange un-whiteness of his own features. An artist must be free to choose what he does, certainly, but he must also never be afraid to do what he might choose.

—Langston Hughes, from "The Negro Artist and the Racial Mountain"

# CONTENTS

## PART 3

## PART 4

# PART 5

# PART 6
## Cocko' the World
### The Incomplete Work with Duke Ellington

# PART 7

# INTRODUCTION

## by Danez Smith

When was the first time you read Langston Hughes? For me, it was seventh or eighth grade English class. During the poetry unit, we read dead poet after dead poet, assigned to analyze these verses to prove we could understand poetry. We were asked to approach poetry as a series of right or wrong interpretations, an act of decoding, maneuvering through English that often felt completely alien from what we spoke. Sometimes we just found ourselves bored. It wasn't a curriculum designed for us to fall in love with poetry, so I didn't.

I left that class thinking all poets were dead, that all the poems had already been written, that most of the poets had been white. A few lines from one of the

pieces we read did stick with me: "I've known rivers,"
Langston Hughes wrote in "The Negro Speaks of
Rivers." He was the only Black poet we studied, and
the title made me think of church, about my pastor's
sermons and all the songs we'd sing about knowing:
knowing Jesus, knowing the way through the storm,
knowing joy will come in the morning. That a short,
quiet poem, one buried deep in a textbook and placed
before me as an uninterested twelve- or thirteen-year-
old, could send my mind to the music and rapture
was new for me. I didn't fall in love with poems then,
but it was my first clue that they might hold some
mighty and transformative power, that they may be
something akin to church; they may change your life.

The next time Hughes loomed large in my life
was my freshman year in college. My friend Sofia
Snow and I had been tasked to remix "Harlem" by
Hughes for our poetry slam team. We were eighteen
years old, and had fallen in love with the power of
spoken word poetry and the electricity of performing
it onstage. We were real serious writers in our minds,
and like many real serious writers before us, we were
seeking inspiration.

We created poetry and choreography in an attempt to answer Hughes's famous question, "What happens to a dream deferred?" In his poems, Hughes showed us that a dream could dry, fester, run, stink, crust and sugar over, and even explode. We stretched our minds to meet Hughes's imagination. With our bodies, we aimed toward our own dreams. We saw our dreams drown, soar, battle, dance, starve, melt, and wait.

Our work in Hughes's shadow exploded with more cringe than genius, yet gave us a chance to imagine our lives through the lens of a master poet. I envied Hughes's brilliance, packed into just a few lines. I searched his poems for more insight about me. I read his words looking for any proof of his queerness while I was still coming into my own, astounded and frustrated that there were only moments where I might speculate, but no hard proof. Hughes might have envied me—the time, ability, and space I have as a poet today to be fully me.

For Hughes, I wrote poems in the voice of his imagined lover. I became hungry to know his beloved Harlem. I read the poets and writers he wrote alongside and called his friends. I listened to the jazz music that made his poetry come alive, and let it enliven me. Not only did I crave his treasure trove of genius but the power of community he sparked around Black lives and artistry. In Hughes's Harlem, there's a wild, queer, and loving brood of Black artists, each one talented and each one aware of art's potential to break open the world. Hughes lived this and it is felt in his poems.

Working on *Blues in Stereo*, I was able to spend time with Langston Hughes's work like never before. He walked me into poetry as a middle schooler and has not let me go. In this collection of his early works, we see his journey, not yet the literary giant but just a boy falling in love with poetry as generations have with his.

In the summer of 1920, an eighteen-year-old Hughes headed to Mexico to live with his father and convince him to provide the money he might use to enroll in Columbia University and become a poet. Somewhere outside St. Louis, on his way to Mexico, Hughes looked out the train window and saw the great Mississippi River. In his first autobiography, 1940's *The*

*Big Sea*, Hughes details for us the story behind his poem "The Negro Speaks of Rivers," what I now wholly recognize as Hughes's most famous poem and one of the most monumental works of verse in the American canon. Hughes recounts about the writing of that poem:

> *I began to think what that river, the old Mississippi, had meant to Negroes in the past....Then I began to think about other rivers in our past—the Congo, and the Niger, and the Nile in Africa—and the thought came to me: "I've known rivers," and I put it down on the back of an envelope I had in my pocket, and within the space of ten or fifteen minutes, as the train gathered speed in the dusk, I had written this poem, which I called "The Negro Speaks of Rivers."*

Consider the making of the poem, the magnitude of this moment, the thoughts that lead up to and the ten or so minutes it took this eighteen-year-old boy to write one of the most known English poems of the twentieth century. Even as a boy, and in the face of a world around him that was built on the hatred against Black people, Hughes chose to love his people nonetheless. The boy loved their music, their beauty, their struggle and ingenuity, their ways of being, their terrors and their graces—so much that it made him want to write a poem.

I'm moved by Hughes, at eighteen, writing a poem where his "I" is big enough to hold all of us, where "The Negro" is both individual and all Black folks. I love that Hughes pointed his words at his people, that he loved Black people and Blackness at a time when that love was largely rejected, and that his poems tell us so. I love that this young man—"that baby," as I'm sure many women called him in those years—wrote *his seminal* poem on an envelope looking out the window in transit.

"The Negro Speaks of Rivers" would go on to be Hughes's first published poem in June 1921, published alongside the bulk of his early work in *The Crisis*, the NAACP's monthly magazine, edited at the time by W. E. B. DuBois. I find myself so moved when I think of a young Hughes finding favor in the eyes of DuBois, his poems featured so abundantly and lovingly in a magazine presented to the people as food for Black people's advancement. *Blues in Stereo* starts there, in the pages of *The Crisis*, where Hughes, too, began.

In your hands is a collection of works from the early writing life of Langston Hughes. When I read the poems in this collection, I feel the gravity of the great attention Hughes paid when looking at his people, and the power encapsulated in that attention. Hughes's influence continues to echo through poetry, fiction, and theater. I would even say that his jazz poems are an ancestor to rap and hip-hop. Artists across genres—writers, musicians, playwrights, and yes, the young slam poets—continue to play in his long shadow every time we exact the musicality of our work, when we transform our language with the possibilities of song, when we proudly claim our people's being and liberation across race, gender, and class as the mission of our craft.

*Blues in Stereo* spans Hughes's adolescent writings, penned between 1921 and 1927. The pieces herewith are uncollected poems, songs, drafts from abandoned projects, and works published in groundbreaking radical Black publications in the

1920s and '30s that are now out of print. In curating this volume, I have strived to maintain the original formatting. I have noted with asterisks areas where Hughes's handwritten notes are unintelligible, and I have maintained his typewriter markings, the X-ing out of lines to reflect the works in progress. Together these early works weave a rich tapestry revealing a young, brilliant, hungry mind that is on fire with a song for Black people; an artist who spoke of the beauty, splendor, and sorrows of the world and bore witness to how those beauties, splendors, and sorrows emanate from and around Black people and refracted across the nation. In publishing them together, these poems, stories, and verses filled with love and favor will echo through history as long as there are humans around to read them.

I hope *Blues in Stereo* sings to you with the same strength and youthful timbre that the archives of Langston Hughes did to me. I found myself swimming in song—verses that made me dance with joy on my mind and songs that left me crying from their quiet and ferocious thunder. A little over a hundred years since Hughes looked out that train window to a river and forever changed the canon of poetry, let us together wade deeper into his work and see again how this young Black man who loved his people changed the history and sound of American poetics.

# PART 1

never stray too far from the question of love and how, indeed, love was a radical and inflamed passion of Hughes. How do these poems transform the world by loving whom they hold? Many of Hughes's early works leave me wandering inside his radical hopes, his dreams, and a sight of the racist, capitalist world around him. I think Hughes is showing us across this set of poems that the work of liberation starts always as an act of care, of loving and seeing someone in the full expression of their being.

# A SONG TO A NEGRO
# WASH-WOMAN

Oh, wash-woman,
Arms elbow-deep in white suds,
Soul washed clean,
Clothes washed clean,—
I have many songs to sing you
Could I but find the words.

Was it four o'clock or six o'clock on a winter
afternoon, I saw you wringing out the last
shirt in Miss White Lady's kitchen? Was it
four o'clock or six o'clock? I don't remember.

But I know, at seven one spring morning you were
on Vermont Street with a bundle in your arms
going to wash clothes.
And I know I've seen you in a New York subway
train in the late afternoon coming home from
washing clothes.

Yes, I know you, wash-woman.
I know how you send your children to school, and
    high-school, and even college.
I know how you work and help your man when
    times are hard.
I know how you build your house up from the
    wash-tub and call it home.
And how you raise your churches from white suds
    for the service of the Holy God.

And I've seen you singing, wash-woman. Out in
    the backyard garden under the apple trees,
    singing, hanging white clothes on long lines in
    the sun-shine.
And I've seen you in church a Sunday morning
    singing, praising your Jesus, because some day
    you're going to sit on the right hand of the Son
    of God and forget you ever were a wash-woman.
    And the aching back and the bundles of clothes
    will be unremembered then.
Yes, I've seen you singing.

And for you,
O singing wash-woman,
    For you, singing little brown woman,
    Singing strong black woman,
    Singing tall yellow woman,
    Arms deep in white suds,
    Soul clean,
    Clothes clean,—
    For you I have many songs to make
    Could I but find the words.

# MOTHER TO SON

Well, son, I'll tell you:
Life for me ain't been no crystal stair.
It's had tacks in it,
And splinters,
And boards torn up,
And places with no carpet on the floor—
Bare.
But all the time
I'se been a-climbin' on,
And reachin' landin's,
And turnin' corners,
And sometimes goin' in the dark
Where there ain't been no light.
So boy, don't you turn back.
Don't you set down on the steps
'Cause you finds it's kinder hard.
Don't you fall now—
For I'se still goin', honey,
I'se still climbin',
And life for me ain't been no crystal stair.

# THE NEGRO SPEAKS OF RIVERS

I've known rivers:

I've known rivers ancient as the world and older
    than the
        flow of human blood in human veins.

My soul has grown deep like the rivers.

I bathed in the Euphrates when dawns were young.
I built my hut near the Congo and it lulled me to
    sleep.
I looked upon the Nile and raised the pyramids
    above it.
I heard the singing of the Mississippi when Abe
    Lincoln
        went down to New Orleans, and I've seen its
muddy
        bosom turn all golden in the sunset.

I've known rivers:
Ancient, dusky rivers.

My soul has grown deep like the rivers.

# YOUNG PROSTITUTE

Her dark brown face
Is like a withered flower
On a broken stem.
Those kind come cheap in Harlem
So they say.

# DREAM VARIATION

To fling my arms wide
In some place of the sun,
To whirl and to dance
Till the white day is done.
Then rest at cool evening
Beneath a tall tree
While night comes on gently,
    Dark like me,—
That is my dream!

To fling my arms wide
In the face of the sun,
Dance! whirl! whirl!
Till the quick day is done.
Rest at pale evening....
A tall, slim tree....
Night coming tenderly
    Black like me.

# PROEM

[Originally published as "The Negro"]

I am a Negro:
>    Black as the night is black,
>    Black like the depths of my Africa.

I've been a slave:
>    Caesar told me to keep his door-steps clean.
>    I brushed the boots of Washington.

I've been a worker:
>    Under my hand the pyramids arose.
>    I made mortar for the Woolworth Building.

I've been a singer:
>    All the way from Africa to Georgia
>    I carried my sorrow songs.
>    I made ragtime.

I've been a victim:
>    The Belgians cut off my hands in the Congo.
>    They lynch me now in Texas.

I am a Negro:
Black as the night is black,
Black like the depths of my Africa.

# POEM

The night is beautiful,
So the faces of my people.

The stars are beautiful,
So the eyes of my people.

Beautiful, also, is the sun.
Beautiful, also, are the souls of my people.

# LAMENT FOR DARK PEOPLES

I was a red man one time,
But the white men came.
I was a black man, too,
But the white men came.

They drove me out of the forest.
They took me away from the jungles.
I lost my trees.
I lost my silver moons.

Now they've caged me
In the circus of civilization.
Now I herd with the many—
Caged in the circus of civilization.

# MY PEOPLE

Dream-singers,
Story-tellers,
Dancers,
Loud laughers in the hands of Fate—
    My People.
Dish-washers,
Elevator-boys,
Ladies' maids,
Crap-shooters,
Cooks,
Waiters,
Jazzers,
Nurses of babies,
Loaders of ships,
Porters,
Hairdressers,
Comedians in vaudeville
And band-men in circuses—
Dream-singers all,
Story-tellers all.
Dancers—

God! What dancers!
Singers—
God! What singers!
Singers and dancers,
Dancers and laughers.
Laughers?
Yes, laughers....laughers.....laughers—
Loud-mouthed laughers in the hands of Fate.

# PART 2

*Because my mouth*
*Is wide with laughter,*
*You do not hear*
*My inner cry,*
*Because my feet*
*Are gay with dancing,*
*You do not know*
*I die.*

n these poems, Hughes's obsessions with music, nightlife, and performers help him illuminate the choreographies of Black life. Undoubtedly, one of Hughes's major projects aims to provide his subjects with pride and dignity, rejecting classist, regressive ideas of the time that sought to privilege the advancement and installation of a privileged and polished Black few instead of making space for all manners of Blackness. In "Minstrel Man" Hughes extends kindness toward the minstrel performer, whom one could easily berate for his wide smile and gay dancing, but Hughes cuts right to what is difficult and private for the speaker. In doing so, Hughes returns to him a dignity from his self-humiliating profession.

Indeed, the shapes and sounds of Black folks take up glorious room in Hughes's work, particularly in his jazz poems, which blur the line between song and poem. Taking their rhythms and structures from gospel, jazz, and the blues, the musical poems of Hughes can be danced and sung as much as they can be read. I feel tambourines and drums close to me when I read "Prayer Meeting":

*Glory! Hallelujah!*
*The dawn's a-comin'!*
*Glory! Hallelujah!*
*The dawn's a-comin'!*

Just as I feel the swing of Harlem when I read "Jazzonia":

*Oh, singing tree!*
*Oh, shining rivers of the soul!*

*Were Eve's eyes*
*In the first garden*
*Just a bit too bold?*

# MINSTREL MAN

Because my mouth
Is wide with laughter
And my throat
Is deep with song,
You do not think
I suffer after
I have held my pain
So long.

Because my mouth
Is wide with laughter,
You do not hear
My inner cry,
Because my feet
Are gay with dancing,
You do not know
I die.

# SONG FOR A BANJO DANCE

Shake your brown feet, honey,
Shake your brown feet, chile,
Shake your brown feet, honey,
Shake 'em swift and wil'
    Get way back, honey,
    Do that low-down step.
    Walk on over, darling,
        Now! Come out
        With your left.
Shake your brown feet, honey,
Shake 'em, honey chile.

Sun's going down this evening—
Might never rise no mo'.
The sun's going down this very night
Might never rise no mo'—
So dance with swift feet, honey,
    (The banjo's sobbing low)
Dance with swift feet, honey—
    Might never dance no mo'.

Shake your brown feet, Liza,
Shake 'em, Liza, chile,
Shake your brown feet, Liza,
    (The music's soft and wil')
Shake your brown feet, Liza,
    (The banjo's sobbing low)
The sun's going down this very night
Might never rise no mo'.

# JAZZONIA

Oh, silver tree!
Oh, shining rivers of the soul!

In a Harlem cabaret
Six long-headed jazzers play.
A dancing girl whose eyes are bold
Lifts nigh a dress of silken gold.

Oh, singing tree!
Oh, shining rivers of the soul!

Were Eve's eyes
In the first garden
Just a bit too bold?
Was Cleopatra gorgeous
In a gown of gold?

Oh, shining tree!
Oh, silver rivers of the soul!

In a whirling cabaret
Six long-headed jazzers play.

# NEGRO DANCERS

"Me an' ma baby's
Got two mo' ways,
Two mo' ways to do de buck!
    Da, da,
    Da, da, da!
Two mo' ways to do de buck!"

Soft light on the tables,
Music gay,
Brown-skin steppers
In a cabaret.

White folks, laugh!
White folks, pray!

"Me an' ma baby's
Got two mo' ways,
Two mo' ways to do de buck!"

# CABARET

Does a jazz-band ever sob?
They say a jazz-band's gay.
Yet as the vulgar dancers whirled
And the wan night wore away,
One said she heard the jazz-band sob
When the little dawn was grey.

# YOUNG SINGER

One who sings "*chansons vulgaires*"
In a Harlem cellar
Where the jazz-band plays
From dark to dawn
Would not understand
Should you tell her
That she is like a nymph
For some wild faun.

# PRAYER MEETING

Glory! Hallelujah!
The dawn's a-comin'!
Glory! Hallelujah!
The dawn's a-comin'!
A black old woman croons in the amen-corner of
    the Ebecaneezer Baptist Church.
A black old woman croons—
The dawn's a-comin'!

# HARLEM NIGHT CLUB

Sleek black boys in a cabaret.
Jazz-band, jazz-band,—
Play, plAY, PLAY!
Tomorrow....who knows?
Dance today!

White girls' eyes
Call gay black boys.
Black boys' lips
Grin jungle joys.

Dark brown girls
In blond men's arms.
Jazz-band, jazz-band,—
Sing Eve's charms!

White ones, brown ones,
What do you know
About tomorrow
Where all paths go?

Jazz-boys, jazz-boys,—
Play, PlAY, PLAY!
Tomorrow....is darkness.
Joy today!

# PART 3

While Harlem may come to mind first when we think of a young Hughes, there are many landscapes that shine in his early works. Hughes's time in the American South, in Mexico, through the Caribbean, and in Africa as a sailor populate his poems with different backgrounds, patterns, and colors. In tandem, as he travels the world, one can see his mind and vision broaden as he understands more about the world, the beauty within it, and its persistent anti-Blackness, offering landscapes to refine his experience and fresh vantage points from which to write.

# THE SOUTH

The lazy, laughing South
With blood on its mouth.
The sunny-faced South,
    Beast-strong,
    Idiot-brained.
The child-minded South
Scratching in the dead fire's ashes
For a Negro's bones.
    Cotton and the moon,
    Warmth, earth, warmth,
    The sky, the sun, the stars,
    The magnolia-scented South.
Beautiful, like a woman,
Seductive as a dark-eyed whore,
    Passionate, cruel,
    Honey-lipped, syphilitic—
    That is the South.
And I, who am black, would love her
But she spits in my face.
And I, who am black,
Would give her many rare gifts

But she turns her back upon me.
    So now I seek the North—
    The cold-faced North,
    For she, they say,
    Is a kinder mistress,
And in her house my children
May escape the spell of the South.

# SEASCAPE

Off the coast of Ireland
    As our ship passed by
We saw a line of fishing ships
    Etched against the sky.

Off the coast of England
    As we rode the foam
We saw an Indian merchantman
    Coming home.

# CARIBBEAN SUNSET

God having a hemorrhage,
Blood coughed across the sky,
Staining the dark sea red,
That is sunset in the Caribbean.

# MEXICAN MARKET WOMAN

This ancient hag
Who sits upon the ground
Selling her scanty wares
Day in, day round,
Has known high wind-swept mountains,
And the sun has made
Her skin so brown.

# THE WHITE ONES

I do not hate you,
For your faces are beautiful, too.
I do not hate you,
Your faces are whirling lights of loveliness and
    splendor, too.
Yet why do you torture me,
O, white strong ones,
Why do you torture me?

# GODS

The ivory gods,
And the ebony gods,
And the gods of diamond and jade,
Sit silently on their temple shelves
While the people
Are afraid.
Yet the ivory gods,
And the ebony gods,
And the gods of diamond-jade,
Are only silly puppet gods
That the people themselves
Have made.

# OUR LAND

### (Poem for a Decorative Panel)

We should have a land of sun,
Of gorgeous sun,
And a land of fragrant water
Where the twilight is a soft bandanna
    handkerchief
Of rose and gold,
And not this land where life is cold.

We should have a land of trees,
Of tall thick trees,
Bowed down with chattering parrots
Brilliant as the day,
And not this land where birds are grey.

Ah, we should have a land of joy,
Of love and joy and wine and song,
And not this land where joy is wrong

Oh, sweet, away!
Ah, my beloved one, away!

# PART 4

Often we see Hughes turn to labor as a site of inquiry. Indeed, all throughout these poems we see people at work thriving, suffering, experiencing a spectrum of emotions from peace to peril. While Hughes would officially deny any affiliation to the Communist Party, he did express an attraction to Communist ideas. Was Hughes's attention to work an expression of solidarity with the working class, or was it simply a requirement to witness labor and laborers if he was to witness the world fully? What did Hughes see in his America that drove him to consider alternate ways of thinking and organizing? What tied his poetry and his politics? In these poems, we may find clues to an answer.

# RAILROAD AVENUE

Dusk dark
On Railroad Avenue.
Lights in the fish joints,
Lights in the pool rooms.
A box car some train
Has forgotten
In the middle of the block.
A player piano,
A victrola.
        942
        Was the number.
A boy
Lounging on the corner.
A passing girl
With purple powdered skin.
        Laughter
        Suddenly
        Like a taut drum.
        Laughter
        Suddenly

Neither truth nor lie.

Laughter

Hardening the dusk dark evening.

Laughter

Shaking the lights in the fish joints,

Rolling white balls in the pool rooms,

And leaving untouched the box car

Some train has forgotten.

# ELEVATOR BOY

I got a job now
Runnin' an elevator
In the Dennison Hotel in Jersey,
Job aint no good though.
No money around.
    Jobs are just chances
    Like everything else.
    Maybe a little luck now,
    Maybe not.
    Maybe a good job sometimes:
    Step out o' the barrel, boy.
Two new suits an'
A woman to sleep with.
    Maybe no luck for a long time.
    Only the elevators
    Goin' up an' down,
    Up an' down,
    Or somebody else's shoes
    To shine,
    Or greasy pots in a dirty kitchen.

I been runnin' this
Elevator too long.
Guess I'll quit now.

# TO CERTAIN INTELLECTUALS

You are no friend of mine
For I am poor.
Black.
Ignorant and slow,—
Not your kind.
You yourself
Have told me so,—
No friend of mine.

# STEEL MILLS

The mills
That grind and grind,
That grind out new steel
And grind away the lives
Of men.—
In the sunset
Their stacks
Are great black silhouettes
Against the sky.
In the dawn
They belch red fire.
The mills.—
Grinding out new steel.
Old men.

# PART 5

fall to the ground at the simplicity of little songs like the poem "The Poppy Flower," which in full reads:

*A wild poppy-flower*
    *Withered and died.*

*The day-people laughed—*
    *But the night-people cried.*

*A wild poppy-flower*
    *Withered and died.*

I know the grief of those night-people, who cry for flowers and make *that* music and move their bodies *that* way. Hughes's poems in *The Crisis* and elsewhere quilt together a world where Black folks are musical, mythical, revered, and adored. From this musical place Hughes waxes brilliantly on grief, intimacy, love, beauty, and many other large, human feelings that poets have wrestled with for centuries. These next poems show Hughes thinking across an array of topics, demonstrating a breadth of possibility in his early work to turn his attention and ever-sharpening skills in any direction he'd like. Two poems here Hughes published under the pseudonym J. Crutchfield Thompson, one of which is in the voice of a dead man. What is it about these poems that made Hughes decide to distance himself, or what was he trying to say through this mask? Was he trying to prove that it was still his skill, not his name or popularity, that made the poems sing?

# BROTHERS

We are related—you and I.
You from the West Indies,
I from Kentucky.
We are related—you and I.
You from Africa,
I from these States.
We are brothers—you and I.

# FASCINATION

Her teeth are as white as the meat of an apple,
Her lips are like dark ripe plums.
I love her.
Her hair is a midnight mass, a dusky aurora.
I love her.
And because her skin is the brown of an oak leaf in
    autumn, but a softer color,
I want to kiss her.

# FIRE-CAUGHT

The gold moth did not love him
So, gorgeous, she flew away.
But the gray moth circled the flame
    Until the break of day.
And then, with wings like a dead desire,
She fell, fire-caught, into the fire.

# MY BELOVED

Shall I make a record of your beauty?
Shall I write words about you?
Shall I make a poem that will live a thousand years
    and paint you in the poem?

# POEM

## (To F. S.)

I loved my friend.
He went away from me.
There's nothing more to say.
The poem ends,
Soft as it began,
I loved my friend.

# SONG FOR A SUICIDE

Oh, the sea is deep
And a knife is sharp
And a poison acid burns;
But they all bring rest
In a deep, long sleep
For which the tired soul yearns—
They all bring rest in a nothingness
From where no road returns.

# POEM

I am waiting for my mother.
She is Death.
Say it very softly.
Say it very slowly if you choose.
I am waiting for my mother,
Death.

# THE POPPY FLOWER

A wild poppy-flower
Withered and died.

The day-people laughed—
But the night-people cried.

A wild poppy-flower
Withered and died.

# SHADOWS

We run,
We run,
We cannot stand these shadows!
Give us the sun.

We were not made
For shade,
For heavy shade,
And narrow space of stifling air
That these white things have made.
We run,
Oh, God,
We run!
We must break through the shadows,
We must find the sun.

# AUTUMN NOTE

The little flowers of yesterday
Have all forgotten May.
The last gold leaf
Has turned to brown.
The last bright day is grey.
The cold of winter comes apace
And you have gone away.

(Published under the pseudonym
J. Crutchfield Thompson)

# EPITAPH

Within this grave I lie,
Yes, I.
Why laugh, good people,
Or why cry?
Within this grave
Lies nothing more
Than I.

(Published under the pseudonym
J. Crutchfield Thompson)

# THE NAUGHTY CHILD

The naughty child
Who ventured to go cut flowers,
Fell into the mill-pond
And was drowned.
But the good children all
Are living yet,
Nice folks now
In a very nice town.

# POEM FOR YOUTH

Raindrops
On the crumbling walls
Of tradition,
Sunlight
Across mouldy pits
Of yesterday.

Oh,
Wise old men,
What do you say
About the fiddles
And the jazz
And the loud Hey! Hey!
About the dancing girls,
And the laughing boys,
And the Brilliant lights,
And the blaring joys,
The firecracker days
And the nights,—
Love-toys?

Staid old men,
What do you say
About sun-filled rain
Drowning yesterday?

# YOUTH

We have tomorrow
Bright before us
Like a flame

Yesterday
A night-gone thing,
A sun-down name.

And dawn to-day
Broad arch above the road we came.

We march!

# LULLABY

(For a Black Mother)

My little dark baby,
My little earth-thing,
My little love-one,
What shall I sing
For your lullaby?
    Stars,
    Stars,
    A necklace of stars
    Winding the night.

My little black baby,
My dark body's baby,
What shall I sing
For your lullaby?
    Moon,
    Moon,
    Great diamond moon,
    Kissing the night.

Oh, little dark baby,
Night black baby,

> Stars, stars,
>
> Moon,
>
> Night stars,
>
> Moon,
>
> For your sleep-song lullaby!

# TO BEAUTY

To worship
At the altar of Beauty,
To feel her loveliness and pain,
To thrill
At the wonder of her gorgeous moon
Or the sharp, swift, silver swords
Of falling rain.

To walk in a golden garden
When an autumn sun
Has almost set,
When near-night's purple splendor
Shimmers to a star-shine net.

To worship
At the altar of Beauty
Is a pleasure divine,
Not given to the many many
But to fools
Who drink Beauty's wine.
Not given to the many many
But to fools

Who seek no other goddess
Nor grapes
Plucked from another's
Vine.

# PART 6

# COCKO' THE WORLD
## The Incomplete Work
## with Duke Ellington

Collected here are drafts from an unfinished collaboration with Duke Ellington called "Cocko' the World," a musical play the two shortly worked on together. Though incomplete, "Cocko' the World" showcases the musical talents of Hughes meeting his great capacity for narrative. The play and its supporting material seem to draw heavily from Hughes's time as a sailor in Africa and Europe. These pieces in particular allow us to witness evidence of him thinking, failing, and digging his way toward an idea that, unfortunately, never saw the light of day during his time. But as they now make their way into the world, I feel blessed by Hughes to have another, more raw, inside look at the creative capacity of one of our legends.

# COCKO' THE WORLD

My pockets may be (is) empty,
There are be holes in my shoes,
But I gets rainbow round my shoulder
And a knockout for the blues.
I'm Cocko' the World, that's me!

I never has no money
But I always has a girl.
I'll tell everybody I'm
Cocko' The World! Cocko the World, that's me!

I ain't no duke for king.
I surely ain't no earl.
I'm just a high-steppin' papa named
Cocko' the World! Cocko' the World, that's me!

My skin ain't white
And my hair's too short to curl—
But I got what it takes
To make me Cocko' the World.

My Face is (black as) just like midnight.
Each tooth is like a pearl—
But my lighthouse smile makes me
Cocko' The World! Cocko' the World, that's me!

I'm a southern sweet potato,
XXX Clark Gable to my girl,
Joe Louis to the men folks,
Called Cocko' the World! Cocko the World,
    that's me!

    I'm a African prince, I'm a dusky pearl,
    I'm a do-nothing duke, I'm Cocko the World!
    I'm a strutter, I'm a dancer,
    A cake-walkin' prancer!
    I'm a lover, I'm a liver,
    A big-hearted giver!
    A smoker and a stoker,
    A loud-laughing joker!
    A rover, a bum,
    My mammy's sugar plum!
    I'm a African prince, a dusky pearl,
    A do-nothing duke,

Called Cocko' the World!
Cocko! Cocko! Cocko' the World!
That's me!

I sing a little song and
I laugh a little while,
Life ain't nothin', folkes,
But a great big smile.
I'm Cocko' the World.

When the road is rocky
I (walk) travels in the field.
If I stub my toe,
I walk on my heel,
I'm Cocko the World, that's me.

When XXXXXXXXXX Gabriel sends the (his)
    chariot
I'm gonna yell Swing low,
Here's one happy angel
Getting (ain't) ready to go,
Cocko' the world, that's me!

I go through this world (my life)
With a song for a pass.
I'm gonna keep on singin'
Long as Cocko lasts.
I'm Cocko on the World,
That's me!

Sometimes I ain't got
No Pillow for my head.
My big black back is my
Only bed.
I'm Cocko' the World, that's me!

Sometimes I don't know
What I'm gonna eat.
Then a crust o' bread
She do taste mighty sweet.
I'm Cocko The world, that's me.

Sometimes I reach up in a tree,
Pull down a leaf that looks like me,
I'm Cocko' the World, that's me, that's me!
Cocko' the world, that's me!

Sometimes I dig down in the sand.
Feels like the world is my left hand.
\*\*\*\*\*\*\*\*

Sometimes I look up in the sky.
Don't grab the (myself a star) sun as I go by.

Sometimes the rain, it fall(s) on me,
And wash me \*\*\*\* (like a) rock in the XXXX
    (deep blue) sea.

My mammy used to look me in the face.
She says (Said), son, (you) make me proud of this
    human race.

Sometimes I gets evil \*\*\*\*\*\* as
I can be
But the good lord knows I don't aim to be.

# COCKO' THE WORLD
## A MUSIC–PLAY

The story of Mammy Bless'em's boy, Cocko, who went out in rags to conquer the world—and came back in rags; found love, found beauty, adventure, gold—and lost them all each time; New Orleans to the West Indies, Port Said, Africa to Paris, finding, losing; but from the broken heart of all his lost dreams, he makes a song—MY SONG—the only thing he brings back home to Mammy.

I.  New Orleans:
    Cocko in the House of Women for Sale,
    where his poor old Mammy serves drinks
    and helps take care of the girls. A steamboat
    whistle blows, and he leaves his sweetheart
    and his mother, to seek his fortune.

II. Ships at Dock:
    Cocko is going to see the world.

III. The Sea:
    Cocko in the galley of the ship where he has
    become a mess-boy; dancing sailors; comedy
    cooks; the entrance to the tropics.

IV. A Land of Rose and Gold;
   The West Indies—monkeys, palms, parrots,
   sunlight, girls—yellow, brown, and black;
   emerald seas, and a SONG OF THE SUN.

V.  Haiti:
   Cocko at a Carnival in the market place;
   Voodoo; THE Congo dancing tropic love.

VI. THE Cock Fight:
   Comedy; luck; then his money goes on a
   black bird that can't fight; and he is broke in
   a strange land.

VII. The Sea again:
   Cocko goes looking for adventure, luck, and
   new love, once more. All the maidens of
   Haiti see him off.


## XXXXX    ACT II    XXXXX

VIII. Paris:
   The flower stalls by the Seine where Cocko
   thinks he meets love in the person of a
   Parisiene prostitute.

IX. The House of Many Mirrors:
   Where all is glitter and the girls are

amazingly lively and gorgeous. But
where Cocko is tricked and deceived, and
everywhere he looks, see himself reflected
in the many mirrors—a fool. He is finally
beaten and thrown out.

X. A Sailors' Cafe at Port Said:
Cocko has taken to drink; everything is
strange, distasteful, and Oriental to him; but
rhum brings back his dreams of home; and
out of the fumes of drugs and licker come
the dancing pickaninnies he used to know.
A great longing comes over him for a place
that would really be home, so he decides to
seek his own Motherland, the black world—
Africa.

XI. A Sandy Sea-coast at the edge of
     the African jungle:
Cocko jumps ship and remains in his home-
land where he believes that at last he will be
free.

XII. The Devil Bush:
He comes unawares upon the young girls in
the secret place where they are being held to
prepare them for marriage.

XIII. The House of the Chief:

> Cocko is given to wife a daughter of the
> royal house, providing he will undergo the
> tribal initiation ceremonies about to be held.

XIV. The Initiation:

> The PUBERTY DANCE, where Cocko,
> with the young men of the tribe, are
> made ready for marriage; then the Test of
> Solitude, where he is left in

XV. The Jungle:

> Alone; a fantasy of beasts and fears; the girl
> he loves comes to him; they attempt to run
> away, but are captured by Arab slave traders
> lurking on the jungle trail.

XVI. Near the Sea:

> The two lovers, in chains, are taken aboard
> ship and carried off to Araby.

XVII. An Arabian Slave Market:

> Cocko and his beloved are sold away from
> one another in the market at Zanzibar.

XVIII. A Colonial Road:

> Cocko laboring on the road in the hot sun.
> All his griefs and pains and troubles come

back to him—and out of them he makes:
MY SONG,—the Negro song of laughter
over pain, of strength out of sorrow.

XIX. The Stoke-Hole at sea.
Cocko is going home, shoveling coal into the
mouths of the red furnaces; the heat and
work overcome him; he faints—beaten at
last by everything.

XX. New Orleans once more:
The House of Women for Sale. Mammy
Bless'em owns the place now. She is very
rich and is about to be married to a *****
young black boy. In the midst of a gorgeous
CAKE-WALK, in comes Cocko—in rags!
But Mammy Bless'em doesn't care how he
looks or what he wears—her boy has come
home, and she is happy. She sings to him as
she did in the first act. And at the end, where
he becomes the step-son of a boy years
younger ***** even than himself, Cocko
sings, beautiful and strong, his song that he
has made up himself, MY SONG; and all
the wedding crowd joins in.

## THE END

# NOTES ON PLAY

Cocko will go to the voodoo house. Up to this time has been able to buy everything he wants. And now that he wants to escape from the voodoo he will want to put money on the altar. But the money will only profane the altar of the voodoo gods.

Cocko hears no English and he is afraid of the African creole. "What are they saying? What do they mean?

Take three scenes and unify—cock fight, carnival and voodoo.

Marseilles—narrow street near the wharf. Cocko could be in bad humor because he has lost all his money, diamond pin, etc. Two or three companions attempt to joke and make merry. Their ardor dampened by his seriousness. They would be discussing ways and means of getting home, but Cocko wants to go to Africa. Before going back to New Orleans he expresses a desire to be with his own people "cross that sea yonder"—across the Mediterranean. Wants to get down there. Complains about everything being "all white, all white" in France. Very serious in this scene. They would begin to sing for the fun of it. "Having got nothing else to do, might as well sing." As they would sing people would occasionally stop and look at them and pass on by. They sing something very familiar to Cocko which he would like so much he would join in. Arouse him out of his bad humor and gradually Cocko falls into humor of crowd. When he begins to sing people stop on the street and look at him. Windows begin to open, etc. Then to their great surprise people begin to throw money, although they had not expected to make any money out of it. Then they really begin to put on a show. Companions might say they would team up and get a lot of money "What's the use of going to Africa"? Cocko: "There you go talking about money, money and I will never get to Africa." He would say that no matter how much money he made he was not going to stay there. He had money in Paris and did not mean anything. Going where the whole world is dark. Goes down toward the docks and his companions shrug their shoulders and follow after him.

Mohammedan scene: All people biblical rather than African. Cocko wants to know where is his

Africa. They say across the desert. Comic idea, little man trying to distinguish people—men and women dressed alike. Oriental music. Narrow street. Net work—trellis. Bazaar. Everybody sells things. Cocko complains that it is worse than Paris or America. Everybody trying to sell something. Wants to see the Africa that is real.

Beachcomber scene: All nationalities. All these people are trying to get ships to go back to civilization from Africa. Last place in the world. No movies, etc. Cocko is the only one going into the interior. Turns on them all. His old boastful self again. What he is going to do in Africa. Going into the interior—the diamond mines. Elephant he is going to bring back to Leota. They all laugh at him.

Dramatic scene: on the wharf. In front of water-front saloon. Ugly scene. Follow it by a very beautiful jungle. All the things he dreamed of—flowers, light, birds. Wanders through this jungle alone. Sailors' saloon. Very terrible white people sitting around talking about civilization and they as examples of it are awful. Spring contrast of jungle scene. Something like in Emperor Jones, except with more light. Sunny jungle. Breaks through this jungle into the devil bush.

The Devil Bush: Cocko breaks into the midst of very beautiful black women. Lovely headdresses, jewels, etc, little clothes as possible. Ivory bracelets. A cry of horror arises from the old ladies, but the maidens are joyful at the sight of a man. The old women rush for help and protection. Pretends not to understand the old women but understands the smiles of the girls and goes toward them. Old women return with men who are not allowed in the bush until girls are taken away. Men come in and take Cocko, bind him with rope and take him to chief. And here he finds himself in his old black land, arrested, arms bound. Place where he expected to be free, not free at all.

Scene in heart of native village: Bamboo throne, very gorgeous. Not in the English manner, but African. Bamboo decorated with ostritch plumes. Cocko brought before throne and the king to his surprise is an Oxford man. When chief comes in, he is wearing ceremonial toga over English business suit. Chief speaks perfect English, but he address Cocko in African, not knowing he is American.

Cocko replies: "I don't know what you are saying, you have to speak to me in something I know." Then chief replies in English. African war dance. Cocko sold into slavery. Big song. Ancestral memories and what Africa means to him in his imagination rather than what he has found it to be. Sings bound as a slave, but the song is of the times when he was free. Cocko is chained to the rest of the slaves. They are considered trophies of victory and therefore part of the dance celebration being held. The chief announces to the tribe that they are to be contracted to the South African owners of the diamond mines. He will make a speech of victory to the tribe. White diamond colonial officials should be there to witness the ceremony—give excuse for the chief to speak in English. And then the victory dance. At the close of the dance the colonial officials, accompanied by native soldiers, depart with the slaves linked one to the other. Cocko last. The little girl with whom he has talked rushes forward with a cry. But is helpless. Look longingly at one another as the human chain drags him to the jungle.

Same jungle scene as formerly but this time instead of being bright and gay, is now full of the sad deep song of the slaves as they pass by.

The diamond mines: Cocko is in the diamond mines. Half fantastic, half real. Voices of the guards—harsh white voices swearing and threatening against black hands touching white diamonds. Silhouette of slaves with picks digging into the earth. Cocko along clearly detached in the foreground. Occasional sparkle of diamond like stones in the blackness. Cocko's scene entirely. He talks of his disappointments, travels—they have amounted to nothing. The diamonds he was going to bring back home to mother and Leota are here but he cannot touch them. They belong to white men. He cannot touch them. "My hands are empty, only my heart is full". Makes up song he is going to take home. Lines: "I have nothing, nothing. only my song." "Out of the earth my song." The song brightens up everything. Diamonds begin to glow. Cocko not African—he is American. The guards would see that he is disturbing influence on the natives working there. They do not dare shoot him—he is an American citizen. So they simply put him out. Tell him to "get out, get out and go". Send him to port town. When he gets there who should be there waiting for him but Sam and Joe. Why have they not gone home? Waiting for him. ***** Ship is there, they will all take it and go home.

Scene where he is sitting and dreaming of home. Dancing girls. He is very tired. In the cafe in Nigeria. The front transparent and he dreams of home and dream of home could be seen through the screen. Sits there all alone. Sees Oriental music—foreign to him. Sits there tired and secs Oriental girls dancing with pomegranates around them. Falls asleep. Girls begin dancing his own kind of music and songs. He is awakened from this by his friends. They could be responsible somewhat for his being released from the diamond mines. Then they go home. He tries to grab Mammy and he grabs Sam. Sam says: "Boy, the boat in coming now." Whistle blows. During the Oriental music you can hear in the distance Sam and Joe singing. As the dream fades and reality comes back the Oriental girls come back. Cocko is bored.

Shipboard scene: Very gay this time. Sailors dance. Very nice dance team. Then New Orleans. Cakewalk. Mardi Gras in New Orleans. Cocko comes with no money. He brings nothing, he says, except his song. He sings his song and impresario contracts him for Broadway and over radio. Mammy not in need of money because she has a beau. Everything all right and very lovely.

# MOON MAGIC

Moon! Oh! moon!
You make me bad.
You drive me mad—
Up there above.
Moon! Haitian moon!
You make me long
For somebody strong
To give me love:
 Oh moon, you make me crazy.
 Everything is hazy.
 Look what you do to me.
 With your light for cover
 I offer to my love;
 All there is of me!
 *Moon! Moon! Moon!*
 Just a Lorelei on a magic isle,
 Love and desire burn in my smile.
 Oh, baby, baby, baby, come and take me soon
 Before I go crazy with the magic of the moon.

# WAR IS WAR

**<u>HERBERT JEWEL:</u>**

(Beside the wreckage of his plane.)

> In time of war 'tis no disgrace
> Should a little accident take place.
> A silly trifle like a falling plane
> Should really cause nobody pain.
> But alas! I believe
> I'm scratched my walking cane!

> ### **<u>Chorus:</u>**
> Oh, war is war! War is war!
> Such odd things can happen
> Since war is war!
> Of course, it's a quite too bad
> That we can't have peace,
> But I really am praying that
> This jolly war won't cease.

## OLD GRANDMA:

(With lipstick and mirror.)

> In time of war 'tis no disgrace
> For an middle-aged woman to paint her face.
> A little powder now and then
> Is what it takes to appeal to man.
> Although I am a grandma and a
>     great-grandma, too.
> Since war is war, soldiers, I'm ready for you.
> (She picks out FROG and flirts with him.)
> ### Chorus:

## FRCO:

> In time of war 'tis no disgrace
> To put on a gas mask and hide your face.
> I'm gonna wear a gas mask to do my kissing
>     through
> Since Listerine in Abbysinia is still taboo
> So come on your garlic eaters,
> What you waiting for?
> I'm all ready for you since war is war.
> ### Chorus:

## COCKO:

(With the Somali girl)

> In time of war 'tis no disgrace
> To do a little hugging in a public place.
> One might even do a little kissing, too,
> So come on, babe, I'm waiting for you.
> Don't hang back and don't get sore.
> You know, sweet sugar, that war is war.
> (Woman drops veil and reveals herself very ugly.)
> ### Chorus:

## STORY:

(Prancing up)

> In time of war 'tis no disgrace
> Should a little mix-up take place
> A silly trifle like a change of sex
> Should really give nobody a pain in the neck.
> Listen, boys, what are you waiting for?
> Come dance with me since war is war.
> ### Chorus:

**BUSTER:**

(Looking scared)

> In time of war 'tis no disgrace
> To run from a bomb at a record pace.
> A silly joker with no sense at all
> Might bare his breast when the bullets fall.
> But I'm gonna run so dog-gone fast
> You can't even see my shadow pass.
> (But I ain't gonna wait for this war to cease.)
>
> ### Chorus:

**DIPLOMAT:**

(With ribbon on breast)

> In time of war 'tis no disgrace
> For folks to use treaties to make Swiss lace.
> A silly trifle like the written word
> Is hardly worth a feather to a bird.
> It's really too bad for a diplomat
> To (have to tell) inform the dove of peace of that.
>
> ### Chorus:

**REPORTER:**

(With pencil and paper at bar-table.)

In time of war 'tis no disgrace
To write a book that's all preface.
From a cafe table near the bar
The front is really not so very far.
But I see no reason to venture that way
As long as I can make the public pay.

**Chorus:**

Oh, war is war! War is war!
Such odd things can happen
Since war is war!
Of course, it's quite too bad
That we can't have peace,
But I really am praying that
This jolly war won't cease.

# A LAND OF SUN

I'll tell the world I don't like the cold.
Zero—zero weather freezes my soul.
But in the tropics the sun is like gold:

>Give me a land of sunlight,
>Let me have a land of joy,
>Where the world is sunbright,
>And everyday's a toy.
>Where great palm trees tower,
>Emerald rivers run,
>And every hour is love's hour
>In a land of sun.

Island of sunlight, little land of fun,
Laughin' and dancing till the day is done—
Everybody's happy livin' in the sun!

>Give me a land of sunlight,
>Let me have a land of joy,
>Where the world is sunbright,

Everyday's a toy.
Where great palm trees tower,
Emerald rivers run,
And every hour is love's hour
In a land of sun.

# SONG OF ADORNMENT

(Devil Bush Scene)

Flowers from the jungles
Peacock feathers
Oils of zanzibar
Leopard's skins
Ivory
Pearls from the Indian shore
Gold
Flamingo's plumes
Ostrich tails
Bushy hair
Flower behind the ear
Lizards claws
Sea shells

Dressed in Moonlight
Dressed in sunlight

Mostly we wear just the air
But sometimes to make the men folks stare
We adorn ourselves with things from everywhere:

# I'LL DROP MY ANCHOR WITH YOU

I'm nothin' but a sailin' rover,
Port to port and town to town.
But now my sailin' days are over
Cause I want to settle down.
Since I've met you, baby dear,
I mean to spend my lifetime here:

    I'm gonna drop my anchor with you.
    No more rovin' will I do.
    Gonna keep my lovin' just for you,
    Night-time and day-time, too.
    I'm tired o' sailin' the ocean wide,
    Pulled and pushed by a lonesome tide.
    Though a girl in every port
    May be a sailor's sport,
    I'd rather have just one girl by my side.
    Your eyes, babe, are a haven
    I know I will be safe in,
    And I can start my life anew.
    So I'm givin' up the sea
    If you'll give yourself to me,
    And let me drop my anchor with you.

# MY LITTLE BLACK DIAMOND

I never had a hundred dollars,
I never had a diamond ring.
But if I had a hundred dollars
I'd buy you a diamond ring.

I'd like to see my girl in diamonds,
XXXXXXXXXXXXXXXXXXXXXXXXXX
Nothing but diamonds.
I'd like to dress my girl in diamonds
From her head to her feet,

XXXXX A sweet brown girl in diamonds
Sure can't be beat.
All I want is
XXXXXXXXXXXXXXXXXXXXXXXXX
XXXXXXXXXX diamonds for my Sallie Lee
XXXXXXXXXXXXXXXXXXXXXXXXX
Cause she's a little XXXXX black diamond to me.
Just a little black diamond to me.

# I OWN THE WORLD

I used to dream about Africa
Everytime I looked at Mobile Bay.
I used to always want to travel
When I saw the blue waves play!

But since you are mine and I am yours
I'll never want another girl.
Since I am yours and you are mine
How you are my world.
I used to dream about another continent,
But now I've gotten ab-solute content,
Since you are mine and I am yours,
Babe, I own the world!

# KALULU

Long ago through the jungles I rode
Strong and black,
Out to the plains on a lion hunt.
I strangled the lions with my own hands,
And carried them home on my back.
King over Africa was I, Kalulu!
When Kalulu said KILL,
The young men killed.
WHEN KALULU said DANCE,
The young girls danced.
The whole jungle trembled at the sound of my
    name.
Then the white men came.
The slave ships came.
They made me a slave.
They took my mother, took my sister,
My sweetheart, my brother,
Away in chai no.
And made me a slave!
I lost you, Lalidjch,

Lost you.
Lost my trees,
I lost my jungle moons.
Now again I am a slave.
Black man **** have made me slave,
King over Africa was I! Kalulu!
Now Kalulu's king no more.

# WORK SONG OF
# THE DIAMOND MINERS

We digs the diamonds, huh!
We digs the gold, huh!
Just like the diamonds, huh!
We's bought and sold, huh!
Bought and sold, huh!
Bought and sold, huh!
Ay, Lawd, huh!
Aw, me; huh!

# AFTER THE SHIP IS GONE

We are the women of the town sailors pay
For an hour, night, or day,
Men with us can have their way.
Yet sometimes there comes
A man we wish would stay———
But he goes,
And we are left alone to say:

    Life is empty, after his ship is gone,
    For sometimes the sailor's love lingers on.
    I wish I was a seagull
    Following his ship to sea.
    Instead, I am left here
    With only a memory.
    A memory of strong arms that held me until
        the dawn.
    Now, I've only the ache of a broken heart—
    After the ship is gone.

# AIRPLANE FACTORIES

I see by the papers
Where the airplane factories still
Don't give much work to colored people—
And it looks like they never will.
Yet it seems mighty funny—
(I don't mean <u>funny</u> to laugh)
That they don't let no colored folks
Work in defense aircraft.
They let naturalized foreigners
And some without first papers
Work most anywhere they want to—
Yet they start to cutting capers
If Negroes apply for jobs,
We're "sabotaging defense"
When we ask for equal rights and try
To get off of Jim Crow's fence.
I don't understand it cause
If we're out for democracy
Why on earth **** Don't they
Give some **** to me?

# PART 7

want to leave you with the poem "Formula," which I know Hughes wants us to take with a good dose of irony. The poem, should we take its claims seriously, are ant-Hughes in their poetics. He's poking fun. Not an ars poetica, but mocking in the voice of "The Muse of Poetry," whom I think is the kind of poet Hughes would least like to see in the world. If not this muse, who will be the poets that speak to the pain? Who will be the poets that grow roses from the dirty, stinky earth? If I can leave you with any call to action, it is to be the artist who can conjure the roses in this poem and who cares for the people around you. I think that would make Hughes content. I believe, like he believed, that poems can help us change the world and we can have an active hand in the matter.

# FORMULA

Poetry should treat
    Of lofty things
Soaring thoughts
    And birds with wings.

The Muse of Poetry
    Should not know
That roses
    In manure grow.

The Muse of Poetry
    Should not care
That earthly pain
    Is everywhere.

Poetry!
    Treat of lofty things:
Soaring thoughts
    And birds with wings.

# CITATIONS

**PART 1**

Hughes, Langston. "A Song to a Negro Wash-Woman." *The Crisis* (Jan. 1925)

Hughes, Langston. "Mother to Son." *The Crisis* (Dec. 1922)

Hughes, Langston. "The Negro Speaks of Rivers." *The Crisis* (June 1921)

Hughes, Langston. "Young Prostitute." *The Crisis* (Aug. 1923)

Hughes, Langston. "Dream Variation." *The Crisis* (July 1924)

Hughes, Langston. "Proem" ["The Negro"]. *The Crisis* (Jan. 1922)

Hughes, Langston. "Poem (The Night is Beautiful)." *The Crisis* (Aug. 1923)

Hughes, Langston. "Lament for Dark Peoples." *The Crisis* (June 1924)

Hughes, Langston. "My People." *The Crisis* (June 1922)

**PART 2**

Hughes, Langston. "Minstrel Man." *The Crisis* (Dec. 1925)

Hughes, Langston. "Song for a Banjo Dance." *The Crisis* (Oct. 1922)

Hughes, Langston. "Jazzonia." *The Crisis* (Aug. 1923)

Hughes, Langston. "Negro Dancers." *The Crisis* (March 1925)

Hughes, Langston. "Cabaret." *The Crisis* (Aug. 1923)

Hughes, Langston. "Young Singer." *The Crisis* (Aug. 1923)

Hughes, Langston. "Prayer Meeting." *The Crisis* (Aug. 1923)

Hughes, Langston. "Harlem Night Club." *The Weary Blues* (New York: Knopf, 1926).

**PART 3**

Hughes, Langston. "The South." *The Crisis* (June 1922)

Hughes, Langston. "Seascape." *The Weary Blues* (New York: Knopf, 1926).

Hughes, Langston. "Caribbean Sunset." *The Weary Blues* (New York: Knopf, 1926).

Hughes, Langston. "Mexican Market Woman." *The Crisis* (March 1922)

Hughes, Langston. "The White Ones." *Opportunity* (March 1924)

Hughes, Langston. "Gods." *The Messenger* (March 1924)

Hughes, Langston. "Our Land (Poem for a Decorative Panel)." *World Tomorrow* (May 1923)

**PART 4**

Hughes, Langston. "Railroad Avenue." *FIRE!!* (Nov. 1926)

Hughes, Langston. "Elevator Boy." *FIRE!!* (Nov. 1926)

Hughes, Langston. "To Certain Intellectuals." *The Messenger* (Feb. 1925)

Hughes, Langston. "Steel Mills." *The Messenger* (Feb. 1925)

**PART 5**

Hughes, Langston. "Brothers." *The Crisis* (Feb. 1924)

Hughes, Langston. "Fascination." *The Crisis* (June 1924)

Hughes, Langston. "Fire-Caught." *The Crisis* (April 1924)

Hughes, Langston. "My Beloved." *The Crisis* (March 1924)

Hughes, Langston. "Poem (To F. S.)." *The Crisis* (May 1925)

Hughes, Langston. "Song for a Suicide." *The Crisis* (May 1924)

Hughes, Langston. "Poem ('I Am Waiting for My Mother...')." *The Crisis* (Aug. 1924)

Hughes, Langston. "The Poppy Flower." *The Crisis*, (Feb. 1925)

Hughes, Langston. "Shadows." *The Crisis* (Aug. 1923)

Hughes, Langston, as J. Crutchfield Thompson. "Autumn Note." *The Messenger* (Sept. 1926)

Hughes, Langston, as J. Crutchfield Thompson. "Epitaph." *The Messenger* (Sept. 1926)

Hughes, Langston. "The Naughty Child." *The Messenger* (June 1927)

Hughes, Langston. "Poem for Youth." *The Messenger* (June 1927)

Hughes, Langston. "Youth." *The Crisis* (August 1924)

Hughes, Langston. "Lullaby." *The Crisis* (March 1926)

Hughes, Langston. "To Beauty." *The Crisis* (Oct. 1926)

### PART 6

Hughes, Langston. "Cocko' the World."
From the Langston Hughes Collection, Yale Collection of American Literature, Beinecke Rare Book and Manuscript Library. Call Number: JWJ MSS 26, Series V, Box 291, folder 4743, Song drafts/typescript holograph and carbon corrected/ n.d.

Hughes, Langston. "Cocko' the World: A Music–Play."
From the Langston Hughes Collection, Yale Collection of American Literature, Beinecke Rare Book and Manuscript Library. Call Number: JWJ MSS 26, Series V, Box 291, folder 4742, Outlines and notes/1928, n.d.

Hughes, Langston. "NOTES ON PLAY."
From the Langston Hughes Collection, Yale Collection of American Literature, Beinecke Rare Book and Manuscript Library. Call Number: JWJ MSS 26, Series V, Box 291, folder 4742, Outlines and notes/1928, n.d.

Hughes, Langston. "Moon Magic."
From the Langston Hughes Collection, Yale Collection of American Literature, Beinecke Rare Book and Manuscript Library. Call Number: JWJ MSS 26, Series V, Box 291, folder 4743, Song drafts/typescript holograph and carbon corrected/ n.d.

Hughes, Langston. "War Is War."
From the Langston Hughes Collection, Yale Collection of American Literature, Beinecke Rare Book and Manuscript Library. Call Number: JWJ MSS 26, Series V, Box 291, folder 4743, Song drafts/typescript holograph and carbon corrected/ n.d.

Hughes, Langston. "Chorus."
From the Langston Hughes Collection, Yale Collection of American Literature, Beinecke Rare Book and Manuscript Library. Call Number: JWJ MSS 26, Series V, Box 291, folder 4743, Song drafts/typescript holograph and carbon corrected/ n.d.

Hughes, Langston. "A Land of Sun."
From the Langston Hughes Collection, Yale Collection of American Literature, Beinecke Rare Book and Manuscript Library. Call Number: JWJ MSS 26, Series V, Box 291, folder 4743, Song drafts/typescript holograph and carbon corrected/ n.d.

Hughes, Langston. "Song of Adornment."
From the Langston Hughes Collection, Yale Collection of American Literature, Beinecke Rare Book and

Manuscript Library. Call Number: JWJ MSS 26, Series V, Box 291, folder 4743, Song drafts/typescript holograph and carbon corrected/ n.d.

Hughes, Langston. "I'll Drop My Anchor with You." From the Langston Hughes Collection, Yale Collection of American Literature, Beinecke Rare Book and Manuscript Library. Call Number: JWJ MSS 26, Series V, Box 291, folder 4743, Song drafts/typescript holograph and carbon corrected/ n.d.

Hughes, Langston. "My Little Black Diamond." From the Langston Hughes Collection, Yale Collection of American Literature, Beinecke Rare Book and Manuscript Library. Call Number: JWJ MSS 26, Series V, Box 291, folder 4743, Song drafts/typescript holograph and carbon corrected/ n.d.

Hughes, Langston. "I Own the World." From the Langston Hughes Collection, Yale Collection of American Literature, Beinecke Rare Book and Manuscript Library. Call Number: JWJ MSS 26, Series V, Box 291, folder 4743, Song drafts/typescript holograph and carbon corrected/ n.d.

Hughes, Langston. "Kalulu." From the Langston Hughes Collection, Yale Collection of American Literature, Beinecke Rare Book and Manuscript Library. Call Number: JWJ MSS 26, Series V, Box 291, folder 4743, Song drafts/typescript holograph and carbon corrected/ n.d.

Hughes, Langston. "Work Song of the Diamond Miners." From the Langston Hughes Collection, Yale Collection of American Literature, Beinecke Rare Book and Manuscript Library. Call Number: JWJ MSS 26, Series V, Box 291, folder 4743, Song drafts/typescript holograph and carbon corrected/ n.d.

Hughes, Langston. "After the Ship Is Gone." From the Langston Hughes Collection, Yale Collection of American Literature, Beinecke Rare Book and Manuscript Library. Call Number: JWJ MSS 26, Series V, Box 291, folder 4743, Song drafts/typescript holograph and carbon corrected/ n.d.

Hughes, Langston. "Airline Factories." From the Langston Hughes Collection, Yale Collection of American Literature, Beinecke Rare Book and Manuscript Library. Call Number: JWJ MSS 26, Series V, Box 373, folder 6105, Drafts/typescript carbon corrected/ n.d.

**PART 7**

Hughes, Langston. "Formula." *The Messenger* (Sept. 1926)

Bringing a book from manuscript to what you are reading is a team effort.

Dialogue Books would like to thank everyone who helped to publish *Blues in Stereo* in the UK.

**Editorial**
Hannah Chukwu
Adriano Noble

**Contracts**
Anniina Vuori
Imogen Plouviez
Amy Patrick
Jemima Coley

**Sales**
Caitriona Row
Dominic Smith
Frances Doyle
Ginny Mašinović
Rachael Jones
Georgina Cutler
Toluwalope Ayo-Ajala

**Design**
Jo Taylor
Nico Taylor

**Production**
Narges Nojoumi

**Publicity**
Millie Seaward

**Marketing**
Emily Moran

**Operations**
Kellie Barnfield
Millie Gibson
Sameera Patel
Sanjeev Braich

**Finance**
Andrew Smith
Ellie Barry